The Book *That* Never Ends

The ABC's to a Highly Effective Life

CAMERON E. PARR

The Holy Bible, New Living Translation - NLT
The Holy Bible, King James Version - KJV
The Holy Bible, New International Version - NIV

Those who profess to favor freedom,
and yet deprecate agitation,
Are men who want crops without
plowing up the ground.
They want rain without thunder and
lightening.
They want the ocean without the
awful roar of its waters.
This struggle may be a moral one;
Or it may be physical one;
Or it may be both moral and physical;
but it must be a struggle.
Power concedes nothing without a demand.
It never did, and it never will.

Frederick Douglass
August 4, 1857

-Excerpt from a speech on West India Emancipation, delivered at Canandaigua (In Quarles 1969, p.354)

DEDICATION

To those who believe earthly recognition and pleasure would fill the void of a broken heart. To those who let their desirous eyes lead their unmovable soul. The individuals who thought worldly success or confirmations were the answers to the peace that passes all understanding. The truth is, the world's unfulfilling rewards hold no truth. We live in a time where the importance of our work drives out the concern for human need. In our work-consumed lives, many things become objects of worship instead of a reminder of whom to worship. This illusory ideology has fooled us into thinking that false idols will grant us joy. Earthly satisfactions have consumed our complex brains with simplicity and mediocrity. Therefore, those who yearn for substance; this book is dedicated to you. This book will provide you with something more precious than silver and gold.

Proverbs 16:16 - How much better to get wisdom than gold and good judgment than silver! (NLT)

The Book that Never Ends....

A

ACTIVATE action. Best described as faith being manifested through hard work. Activation can only be activated by the activator...you! This requires your independent accountability in any area in which you are struggling. Action is the only way to fix any situation that is hindering your growth. Without action, your faith will lay dormant. Spiritual growth gets you into the Promised Land but cleaning up your inner-self gets you closer to The Most High. When you clean up, you become an individual after God's own heart. This is true, because as you do so, you begin to learn how to properly listen for His instructions. When you listen to His instruction, you can openly receive information.

James 2:22 - You see that his faith and his actions were working together, and his faith was made complete by what he did. (NIV)

Acts 13:22 - But God removed Saul and replaced him with David, a man about whom God said, I have found David son of Jesse, a man after my own heart. He will do everything I want him to do. (NLT)

Take a deep breath. Find a mirror.
Read the statement below out loud
and then write down the answer.

I, _____, forgive

myself for _____.

B

Balance and awareness are essential characteristics when traveling on your journey. Therefore be driven, and cultivate every level of self-awareness. The major categories of self-awareness to reflect upon are: (1) Emotional intelligence (2) Personal values (3) Learning style (4) Position towards change, and (5) Individual evaluation. This process of developing self-awareness is the cornerstone of any driving force that consciously exists and executes. Appreciate how balance creates stability, on which an unwavering foundation can be built.

Proverbs 25:16 – If you find honey, eat just enough; too much of it, and you will vomit. (NIV)

Hebrews 13:2 - Don't forget to show hospitality to strangers, for some who have done this have entertained angels without realizing it! (NLT)

Take a deep breath. Find a mirror. Read the statement below out loud and then write down the answer.

I, _____, need to take control of _____.

C

CRY to persevere, not to quit. Shedding tears is often associated with weakness or the inability to express yourself. But contrary to what most people think, it is how you react *after* you cry that defines you. Whether you have to kick, scream, hurt, or endure ... use this very human emotion to push through.

John 11:35 – Jesus wept. (KJV)

James 1:2 - Dear brothers and sisters, when troubles come your way, consider it an opportunity for great joy. (NLT)

Take a deep breath. Find a mirror.
Read the statement below out loud
and then write down the answer.

I, _____, will persevere.

D

DETACH from your old self if you're not seeing growth. Dare yourself to recreate how you treat yourself. By detaching from your old ways and beliefs, you create space to bring in the new and move out the old. Understand that without detaching from toxic behavior, you will continue the cycle of being a hurt person that hurts people. You can't expect different results by reacting the same way to every situation.

Ephesians 4:22-23 – Throw off your old sinful nature and your former way of life, which is corrupted by lust and deception. Instead, let the Spirit renew your thoughts and attitudes. (NLT)

Take a deep breath. Find a mirror.
Read the statement below out loud
and then write down the answer.

I, _____, was never
shown how to properly love.

E

EXTERNALLY being affected cannot break down a strong internal foundation. Today's society focuses on gaining acceptance from external sources. The more you grow and internalize who you are and manifest your purpose, society will viciously try to impede and thwart your growth. The evidence of internal growth is evidenced when others start to recognize that you are "different." The truth is, they see a better person, but they cannot effectively express what they see. Internalize personal development by being the change you want to see. Can you control you?

Galatians 5:19 - Now the works of the flesh are manifest, which are *these*; Adultery, fornication, uncleanness, lasciviousness. (KJV)

Galatians 5:20 - Idolatry, witchcraft, hatred, variance, emulations, wrath, strife, seditions, heresies. (KJV)

Galatians 5:21 - Envying's, murders, drunkenness, revellings, and such like: of which I tell you before, as I have also told *you* in time past, that they which do such things shall not inherit the kingdom of God. (KJV)

Take a deep breath. Find a mirror.
Read the statement below out loud
and then write down the answer.

I, _____, am not over

the fact that _____.

F

FLEXIBLE, just like a rubber band. Most people misconstrue strength with heavy objects. Unlike a heavy object, a rubber band displays the perfect example of strength. Rubber bands hold things together, and they bend and adapt extremely well under pressure. Even when the rubber band snaps from excessive stress, you can mend it back together. The rubber band is enduring and designed to withstand high amounts of strain. Adapt this strategy to your everyday life, especially when life manifests issues beyond your control.

James 3:17 - But the wisdom from above is first of all pure. It is also peace-loving, gentle at all times, and willing to yield to others. It is full of mercy and good deeds. It shows no favoritism and is always sincere. (NLT)

Take a deep breath. Find a mirror. Read the statement below out loud and then write down the answer.

I, _____, am afraid of _____.

G

GOD works on His own time as He addresses your circumstances. Nothing can happen unless The Most High commands it. What may seem unbelievable, impossible, or strange to you is effortless and natural to Him. The ups and downs in your life's journey are strictly designed so that you can acknowledge that it is only through The Most High that all things are possible.

1 Kings 17:4 - Drink from the brook and eat what the ravens bring you, for I have commanded them to bring you food. (NLT)

1 Kings 17:6 - The ravens brought him bread and meat each morning and evening, and he drank from the brook. (NLT)

Take a deep breath. Find a mirror. Read the statement below out loud and then write down the answer.

I, _____, promise
that _____.

H

HELP others but pay yourself first. When you are in a position to manifest your essence and the fruits from your journey, then show others how to obtain the same principles. For example, during an emergency on a plane, you are instructed to put your safety mask on first, then proceed to help others. Help yourself by establishing yourself.

Matthew 5:16 - Let your light so shine before men, that they may see your good works, and glorify your Father which is in heaven. (KJV)

Take a deep breath. Find a mirror.
Read the statement below out loud
and then write down the answer.

I, _____, never told
_____ I love them.

I

INVEST in yourself, and not only financially. Invest in yourself emotionally, mentally, physically, and spiritually. To make an investment means you are willing to sacrifice what you have to obtain a greater return. When you invest and commit in yourself properly, you're guaranteed to receive intangible jewels. Tangible materials quickly lose value, but the fruits of the spirit blossom and multiply. What are you willing to sacrifice to regain your self-worth?

Galatians 5:22-23 - But the fruit of the Spirit is love, joy, peace, longsuffering, gentleness, goodness, faith, meekness, temperance: against such there is no law. (KJV)

Take a deep breath. Find a mirror.
Read the statement below out loud
and then write down the answer.

I, _____, want another

chance to fix _____.

J

JUST do it. No excuses, no procrastination, no missed opportunities. Focus on adjustments instead of excuses in your daily life. By just doing it, you leave the gate of failure wide open, and you confront your biggest fears. To achieve big, you must sacrifice big; jump off the edge and fly. You owe it to yourself to see what you're made of. You can only overcome the fear of flying by flying. Let the world see who you are before the grave swallows you and your dreams forever. "The only thing we have to fear is fear itself." – Franklin D. Roosevelt, March 4, 1933.

Proverbs 18:9 - A lazy person is as bad as someone who destroys things. (NLT)

Take a deep breath. Find a mirror.
Read the statement below out loud
and then write down the answer.

I, _____, failed to give
my all in _____.

K

KNOWLEDGE of self is an underestimated trait in today's world. If you know you struggle in specific areas, circumstances, or situations, then stay away from them until you're strong enough to overcome them. To better obtain knowledge of self, you must understand how you learn. Once you know how you learn, you can utilize this knowledge and apply it in your daily life. Self-knowledge is a jewel because it enables you to acquire insight—and foresight. When acquired properly, you gain the power to avoid the same shortcomings of those around you. Equally, it would behoove you to be careful when you laugh at people who stumble, because no one is exempt from the pitfalls of life.

Ephesians 6:12 - For we wrestle not against flesh and blood, but against principalities, against powers, against the rulers of the darkness of this world, against spiritual wickedness in high places. (KJV)

Proverbs 24:5 - The wise are mightier than the strong and those with knowledge grow stronger and stronger. (NLT)

Take a deep breath. Find a mirror.
Read the statement below out loud
and then write down the answer.

I, _____, run away from
_____, especially when I'm emotional.

L

LOVE conquers all, so it's okay to love people from a distance. The problem with distance is the majority of people mistakenly interpret your distance for negativity. To understand love, it's important to know the different languages of love. The common love languages are: (1) receiving gifts, (2) quality time, (3) words of affirmation, (4) acts of service (devotion), and (5) physical touch. To effectively love yourself and those you care for, find what love language you speak and how you respond to others.

Proverbs 8:21 - That I may cause those that love me to inherit substance; and I will fill their treasures. (KJV)

Matthew 5:44 - But I say unto you, Love your enemies, bless them that curse you, do good to them that hate you, and pray for them which despitefully use you, and persecute you. (KJV)

Take a deep breath. Find a mirror.
Read the statement below out loud
and then write down the answer.

I, _____, love the
person I am becoming.

M

MAINTAIN consistency. There are no shortcuts on the path to success. Focus on your goals and dreams until they become the sole reason why you wake up. Consistency will allow you to clearly see, feel, touch, smell and better hear what you must do to achieve your goals. This holds true because once you know what you want, you will be capable to strategically calculate what needs to be done. Through this process, you can achieve a better understanding of the sweat-to-work ratio you need in order to manifest greatness.

Romans 12:2 - And be not conformed to this world: but be ye transformed by the renewing of your mind, that ye may prove what *is* that good, and acceptable, and perfect, will of God. (KJV)

Proverbs 22:4 - True humility and fear of the LORD lead to riches, honor, and long life. (NLT)

Take a deep breath. Find a mirror.
Read the statement below out loud
and then write down the answer.

I, _____, intentionally ignore
_____ because it's my biggest hurdle.

N

NO apologies for what's burning in your heart, mind, body, and soul to fulfill. This concept applies to those who feel apologetic because their purpose may seem foolish to those around them. Not everyone is going to share your dreams and aspirations. Don't fall for the booby trap by letting these people put a banana in your tailpipe. You don't have to spend 40 years in the wilderness because you're scared your growth is going to offend someone.

Ecclesiastes 9:11 - I have seen something else under the sun: The race is not to the swift or the battle to the strong, nor does food come to the wise or wealth to the brilliant or favor to the learned; but time and chance happen to them all. (NIV)

Take a deep breath. Find a mirror.
Read the statement below out loud
and then write down the answer.

I, _____, have successfully
accomplished _____.

O

ORGANIZE your strengths, weaknesses, and attributes of greatness into categories. If you don't think you're "great" at anything, focus on what you're good at instead. Remember, being good for a long period of time can lead to greatness. If you don't feel like you're good at anything, put extra focus and effort on an area in your life where you're productive. You can never be great by being someone else.

Romans 11:29 - For the gifts and calling of God are without repentance. (KJV)

Romans 12:6 - Having then gifts differing according to the grace that is given to us, whether prophecy, let us prophesy according to the proportion of faith. (KJV)

Take a deep breath. Find a mirror.
Read the statement below out loud
and then write down the answer.

I, _____, am good

at _____.

P

PRODUCTIVE practices protect prior planning. This holds true because you can measure what you have produced compared to what you had initially planned. During your practices, the hard work you invest requires struggle. The pain experienced through the struggle toughens your mind. Strength, endurance, and perseverance can now be birthed. The necessary pain you experience in practice prepares you to accept those circumstances beyond your control. This is important because when hard times come, you will not be affected deeply.

Psalms 1:3 - And he shall be like a tree planted by the rivers of water, that bringeth forth his fruit in his season; his leaf also shall not wither; and whatsoever he doeth shall prosper. (KJV)

*Take a deep breath. Find a mirror.
Read the statement below out loud
and then write down the answer.*

I, _____, dedicate
   myself to _____.

Q

QUIETLY consume your piece of humble pie. Take the silence and peace that is given to you to reflect upon the things you are grateful for. Work in silence to birth a blessing. Silence is golden because it allows your actions to speak loudly. You were given two ears and one mouth, so let your humility be as strong as your greatness.

2 Chronicles 7:14 - If my people, which are called by my name, shall humble themselves, and pray, and seek my face, and turn from their wicked ways; then will I hear from heaven, and will forgive their sin, and will heal their land. (KJV)

Take a deep breath. Find a mirror.
Read the statement below out loud
and then write down the answer.

I, _____, value _____
and love _____.

R

REEL in every achievement and keep it. This is extremely important for when you get discouraged and question your journey. Reeling in allows you to go back and reconnect with what you have already accomplished along the way.

2 John 1:8 - Watch out that you do not lose what we have worked so hard to achieve. Be diligent so that you receive your full reward. (NLT)

Take a deep breath. Find a mirror.
Read the statement below out loud
and then write down the answer.

I, _____, have grown
    because _____.

S

SERVANT-LEADER is the way, because to be effective as a leader, first you must serve. Lead by example and take full responsibility of the outcome, whether good or bad. A servant-leader is humble and understands the value of communication. Effective communication means you speak *to* the problem, not *at* it. As a servant-leader, you want people to pray the same prayers you pray for them.

Luke 22:25-26 - Jesus told them, in this world the kings and great men lord it over their people, yet they are called 'friends of the people. 'But among you it will be different. Those who are the greatest among you should take the lowest rank, and the leader should be like a servant. (NLT)

Take a deep breath. Find a mirror.
Read the statement below out loud
and then write down the answer.

I, _____ will make
adjustments, not excuses.

T

TRUTH be unto you. Spiritual enlightenment isn't the same as self-growth. Focus on being sharp on every corner; emotional, mentally, physically, and spiritually stable. Find useful information to help validate your truth. Without truth, there are only lies and lies only birth more lies. The truth begat accountability, to which accountability begat respect. Accountability and information will allow new beginnings. Truth and knowledge shall set you free.

Proverbs 3:3 - Let not mercy and truth forsake thee: bind them about thy neck; write them upon the table of thine heart. KJV

Take a deep breath. Find a mirror. Read the statement below out loud and then write down the answer.

I, _____, know self-esteem relies upon self.

U

UNLEARN non-rewarding habits that have caused toxicity in your life. These bad habits have mutated and instinctively shaped your mentality to see situations and circumstances in a negative light. By unlearning, you can effectively relearn or replace an old mentality with mature insight. This will enable you to properly attack those situations with which you struggle with confidence and a renewed mind. Once you unlearn, find your specific style of learning. The different types of learning are: (1) Visual (spatial) —you prefer using pictures, images, and spatial understanding; (2) Aural (auditory-musical)—you prefer using sound and music; (3) Verbal (linguistic)— you prefer using words, both in speech and writing; (4) Physical (kinesthetic)—you prefer using your body, hands, and sense of touch. Obtain wisdom, understanding, and knowledge by learning in a way that suits you.

1 Corinthians 13:11 - When I was a child, I spake as a child, I understood as a child, I thought as a child: but when I became a man, I put away childish things. (KJV)

Take a deep breath. Find a mirror.
Read the statement below out loud
and then write down the answer.

I, _____, will break
the negative curses.

V

VACANT places in your past can compel you to become empty in your present life. This is a common behavioral pattern that allows you to be physically present, but mentally, emotionally, or spiritually absent. Moreover, because your emptiness is unchecked, nothing can move in or move out.

Deuteronomy 9:6 - You must recognize that the LORD your God is not giving you this good land because you are good, for you are not—you are a stubborn people. (NLT)

Deuteronomy 10:16 - Therefore, change your hearts and stop being stubborn. (NLT)

Take a deep breath. Find a mirror. Read the statement below out loud and then write down the answer.

I, _____, know asking for help isn't a sign of weakness.

W

WORK on your weak areas until you are comfortable being uncomfortable. Work is an overused term that is thrown around without consequence. In the 24 hours given to you, you should give your last breath to work on yourself. Hard work is painful, but pain is temporary, and it's imperative that you keep going. Get something out of your struggle and pain. The bigger your goals, the harder you must work ... Do a little more every day, and every day work a little harder.

Proverbs 12:14 - Wise words bring many benefits and hard work brings rewards. (NLT)

Proverbs 13:11 - Wealth from get-rich-quick schemes quickly disappears wealth from hard work grows over time. (NLT)

Take a deep breath. Find a mirror.
Read the statement below out loud
and then write down the answer.

I, _____, am willing
to be uncomfortable.

X

XEROX copy is exactly what you are not. You are a unique, one-of-a-kind masterpiece that has a specific task. Though people are plentiful like sand on the beach, you and those around you each contribute to help align and divide land from the sea. No one can fit your tailor-made image. Give birth to your purpose and bless the world with it.

Matthew 10:30-31 - But the very hairs of your head are all numbered. Fear ye not therefore, ye are of more value than many sparrows. (KJV)

Take a deep breath. Find a mirror.
Read the statement below out loud
and then write down the answer.

I, _____, know there
are no short-cuts to success.

Y

YIELDS will appear in your yard. One of the most overlooked aspects is reaping what you have sown. When you look within yourself and survey what you have planted, does your harvest feed you or poison you? Many of the things you have planted within yourselves are not only toxic to you, but also to those who come in contact with you. The majority of yields you have reaped are thrown away or misused, forcing you to replant. This process is not only time consuming, but frustrating as well.

2 Timothy 2:3 - Endure suffering along with me, as a good soldier of Christ Jesus. And as Christ's soldier, do not let yourself become tied up in the affairs of this life, for then you cannot satisfy the one who has enlisted you in this army. Follow the Lord's rules for doing his work, just as an athlete either follows the rules or is disqualified and wins no prize. Hardworking farmers are the first to enjoy the fruit of their labor. (NLT)

Take a deep breath. Find a mirror.
Read the statement below out loud
and then write down the answer.

I, _____, am good

at _____.

Z

ZONE off certain people, places, and practices that do not allow you to grow. Without zoning, you can unconsciously become what you said you'd never want to be. Misery loves company. For example, if you spend time around nine impoverished people, you will soon be the tenth. Zoning will allow you to keep everyone off your front row. When you understand people's intentions and motives, you can easily put them into their proper seating arrangements in regards to your life's priority list.

Ephesians 4:18-19 & 23-27 - Their closed minds are full of darkness; they are far away from the life of God because they have shut their minds and hardened their hearts against him. They don't care anymore about right and wrong, and they have given themselves over to immoral ways. Their eyes are filled with all kinds of impurity and greed. Instead, there must be a spiritual renewal of your thoughts and attitudes. You must display a new nature because you are a new person, created in God's likeness-righteous, holy, and true. So put away all falsehoods and "tell you neighbor the truth" because we belong to each other. And "don't sin by letting anger gain control over you." Don't let the sun go down while you are still angry, for anger gives a mighty foothold to the Devil. (NLT)

*Take a deep breath. Find a mirror.
Read the statement below out loud
and then write down the answer.*

I, _____, will be comfortable, being
uncomfortable to achieve _____.

IT'S OKAY, BECAUSE THIS
BOOK IS REALLY ABOUT ME...

CONCLUSION

This book is designed to help form a bridge between you and your goals. In a short amount of time, you should be able to understand the importance of sacrifice. Furthermore, if internalized correctly, this book will enable you to manifest the true potential that is concealed within you.

Through seeking, knocking, and asking for what is true, change is promised to come. In accepting Christ Jesus, you can effectively prepare to receive the intangible jewels. These jewels are commonly called Fruit of the Spirit; love, peace, self-control, long-suffering, patience, kindness, goodness, faithfulness, gentleness, and joy. Against such, there is no law (Galatians 5:22-23 KJV). The proper understanding of such jewels allows you to bless others while they are here in their physical days. This holds true because it is your purpose to have a positive impact that influences and transforms comfort or contentment in this world. This transition can only be achieved by manifesting the Godly potential that is within you.

Some individuals in your life have to stay in the wilderness because they might spoil your blessings. As life progresses, one should understand that opportunities have an expiration date. The more individuals you have in your life, the easier it is to mistake those who take value away from your life with those who add value. The troubling part is those that take away seldom replace what they have taken.

Made in the USA
Monee, IL
02 October 2023

43815388R00035